may you be proud
of the work you do,
the person you are,
and the difference
you make!

THANK
YOU

for all you do!

THIS NOTEBOOK — JOURNAL BELONGS TO:

"Thank you
For All
You Do!"

/

"Believe in miracles but above all believe in yourself!"

Date: /   /

THINGS TO BE GRATEFUL FOR TODAY

"Let your dreams be as big as your desire to succeed"

Date: /   /

THINGS TO BE GRATEFUL FOR TODAY

Date: /   /

_____
_____
_____
_____
_____
_____
_____
_____
_____
_____
_____
_____
_____
_____
_____
_____
_____
_____
_____

THINGS TO BE GRATEFUL FOR TODAY

> *"They say I dream too big. I say they think too small"* - Unknown

Date: /   /

_____

_____

_____

_____

_____

_____

_____

_____

_____

_____

_____

_____

_____

_____

_____

_____

_____

THINGS TO BE GRATEFUL FOR TODAY

"Never be afraid to start something new, if you fail it is just temporary, if you believe and persist you will succeed"

Date: /   /

_____

_____

_____

_____

_____

_____

_____

_____

_____

_____

_____

_____

_____

_____

_____

_____

_____

THINGS TO BE GRATEFUL FOR TODAY

> *"Your driving force and your power lies within you and the size of your dreams, never give up!"*

Date: /   /
_____

_____
_____
_____
_____
_____
_____
_____
_____
_____
_____
_____
_____
_____
_____
_____
_____
_____
_____

THINGS TO BE GRATEFUL FOR TODAY

> *"Wherever you go, go with all your heart."*
> *- Confucius*

Date: /   /

THINGS TO BE GRATEFUL FOR TODAY

"Never Ever Give Up"

Date: /   /

_____

_____

_____

_____

_____

_____

_____

_____

_____

_____

_____

_____

_____

_____

_____

_____

_____

_____

_____

_____

THINGS TO BE GRATEFUL FOR TODAY

Date: /   /

THINGS TO BE GRATEFUL FOR TODAY

"Never give up, keep going no matter what!"

Date: /   /

THINGS TO BE GRATEFUL FOR TODAY

"Start where you are and take chances"

Date: /   /

_____

_____

_____

_____

_____

_____

_____

_____

_____

_____

_____

_____

_____

_____

_____

_____

_____

_____

_____

THINGS TO BE GRATEFUL FOR TODAY

Date: /   /

_____

_____

_____

_____

_____

_____

_____

_____

_____

_____

_____

_____

_____

_____

_____

_____

_____

_____

THINGS TO BE GRATEFUL FOR TODAY

Date: /   /

THINGS TO BE GRATEFUL FOR TODAY

> *"Change your life today. Don't gamble on the future, act now, without delay."* — Simone de Beauvoir

Date: /   /

_____

_____

_____

_____

_____

_____

_____

_____

_____

_____

_____

_____

_____

_____

_____

_____

_____

_____

THINGS TO BE GRATEFUL FOR TODAY

"Keep your motivation and your momentum with a new goal every day!"

Date: /   /

_____

_____

_____

_____

_____

_____

_____

_____

_____

_____

_____

_____

_____

_____

_____

_____

_____

_____

THINGS TO BE GRATEFUL FOR TODAY

"Aim for the stars to keep your dreams alive"

Date: /   /

_____

_____

_____

_____

_____

_____

_____

_____

_____

_____

_____

_____

_____

_____

_____

_____

_____

_____

THINGS TO BE GRATEFUL FOR TODAY

"When life gives you lemons, add a little gin and tonic"

Date: /   /

THINGS TO BE GRATEFUL FOR TODAY

Date: /   /

_____

THINGS TO BE GRATEFUL FOR TODAY

"When you feel you are defeated, just remember, you have the power to move on, it is all in your mind"

Date: /   /
_____

_____

_____

_____

_____

_____

_____

_____

_____

_____

_____

_____

_____

_____

_____

_____

_____

_____

THINGS TO BE GRATEFUL FOR TODAY

Date: /   /

THINGS TO BE GRATEFUL FOR TODAY

"Opportunity comes to those who never give up"

Date: / /

_____

_____

_____

_____

_____

_____

_____

_____

_____

_____

_____

_____

_____

_____

_____

_____

_____

THINGS TO BE GRATEFUL FOR TODAY

"You are the creator of your own opportunities"

Date: /   /

THINGS TO BE GRATEFUL FOR TODAY

Date: /   /

THINGS TO BE GRATEFUL FOR TODAY

Date: /   /

THINGS TO BE GRATEFUL FOR TODAY

> *"Every achievement starts with
> a dream and a goal in mind"*

Date: /   /

_____

_____

_____

_____

_____

_____

_____

_____

_____

_____

_____

_____

_____

_____

_____

_____

_____

_____

_____

THINGS TO BE GRATEFUL FOR TODAY

Date: /   /

_____

_____

_____

_____

_____

_____

_____

_____

_____

_____

_____

_____

_____

_____

_____

_____

_____

THINGS TO BE GRATEFUL FOR TODAY

> *"Never loose confidence in your dreams, there will be obstacles and defeats, but you will always win if you persist"*

Date: /   /

THINGS TO BE GRATEFUL FOR TODAY

""Never wait for someone else to validate your existence, you are the creator of your own destiny"

Date: /   /

_____

_____

_____

_____

_____

_____

_____

_____

_____

_____

_____

_____

_____

_____

_____

_____

_____

_____

THINGS TO BE GRATEFUL FOR TODAY

"Dreams are the energy that power your life"

Date: /   /

_____

_____
_____
_____
_____
_____
_____
_____
_____
_____
_____
_____
_____
_____
_____
_____

THINGS TO BE GRATEFUL FOR TODAY

"Dreams make things happen, nothing is impossible as long as you believe." - Anonymous

Date: /   /

_____

_____

_____

_____

_____

_____

_____

_____

_____

_____

_____

_____

_____

_____

_____

_____

_____

THINGS TO BE GRATEFUL FOR TODAY

"Always dream big and follow your heart"

Date: /   /

_____

_____

_____

_____

_____

_____

_____

_____

_____

_____

_____

_____

_____

_____

_____

_____

_____

_____

THINGS TO BE GRATEFUL FOR TODAY

"Never stop dreaming." - Anonymous

Date: /   /

_____

_____

_____

_____

_____

_____

_____

_____

_____

_____

_____

_____

_____

_____

_____

THINGS TO BE GRATEFUL FOR TODAY

"Everything you dream is possible as long as you believe in yourself"

Date: /   /

_____

_____

_____

_____

_____

_____

_____

_____

_____

_____

_____

_____

_____

_____

_____

_____

_____

THINGS TO BE GRATEFUL FOR TODAY

"Dream big, it's the first step to success" - Anonymous

Date: /   /

THINGS TO BE GRATEFUL FOR TODAY

"A successful person is someone that understands temporary defeat as a learning process, never give up!"

Date: /   /

_____

_____

_____

_____

_____

_____

_____

_____

_____

_____

_____

_____

_____

_____

_____

_____

_____

_____

THINGS TO BE GRATEFUL FOR TODAY

"Motivation comes from working on our dreams and from taking action to achieve our goals"

Date: /   /

_____

_____

_____

_____

_____

_____

_____

_____

_____

_____

_____

_____

_____

_____

_____

_____

_____

_____

_____

_____

THINGS TO BE GRATEFUL FOR TODAY

"Dreams are the foundation to our imagination and success"

Date: /   /

THINGS TO BE GRATEFUL FOR TODAY

Date: /   /

THINGS TO BE GRATEFUL FOR TODAY

Date: /   /

THINGS TO BE GRATEFUL FOR TODAY

Date: /   /

_____

_____

_____

_____

_____

_____

_____

_____

_____

_____

_____

_____

_____

_____

_____

_____

THINGS TO BE GRATEFUL FOR TODAY

Date: / /

THINGS TO BE GRATEFUL FOR TODAY

> *"Put more energy into your dreams than Into your fears and you will see positive results"*

Date: /   /

_____

_____

_____

_____

_____

_____

_____

_____

_____

_____

_____

_____

_____

_____

_____

_____

_____

THINGS TO BE GRATEFUL FOR TODAY

> *"Let your dreams be bigger than your fears and your actions louder than your words."* - Anonymous

Date: /   /
_____
_____
_____
_____
_____
_____
_____
_____
_____
_____
_____
_____
_____
_____
_____
_____
_____
_____

THINGS TO BE GRATEFUL FOR TODAY

"Always keep moving forward to keep your balance, if you stop dreaming you will fall"

Date: /   /

THINGS TO BE GRATEFUL FOR TODAY

Date: /   /

_____

_____

_____

_____

_____

_____

_____

_____

_____

_____

_____

_____

_____

_____

_____

_____

_____

_____

THINGS TO BE GRATEFUL FOR TODAY

"Dream. Believe. Create. Succeed" - Anonymous

Date: /   /

_____

_____

_____

_____

_____

_____

_____

_____

_____

_____

_____

_____

_____

_____

_____

_____

_____

_____

_____

THINGS TO BE GRATEFUL FOR TODAY

"You are never to old to set new goals and achieve them, keep on dreaming!"

Date: / /

THINGS TO BE GRATEFUL FOR TODAY

> *"If you have big dreams you will always have big reasons to wake up every day"*

Date: /   /

_____

_____

_____

_____

_____

_____

_____

_____

_____

_____

_____

_____

_____

_____

_____

_____

THINGS TO BE GRATEFUL FOR TODAY

"Difficulties are nothing more than opportunities in disguise, keep on trying and you will succeed"

Date: /   /

THINGS TO BE GRATEFUL FOR TODAY

Date: /   /

_____

_____

_____

_____

_____

_____

_____

_____

_____

_____

_____

_____

_____

_____

_____

_____

_____

_____

THINGS TO BE GRATEFUL FOR TODAY

Date: / /

_____

_____

_____

_____

_____

_____

_____

_____

_____

_____

_____

_____

_____

_____

_____

_____

_____

_____

_____

THINGS TO BE GRATEFUL FOR TODAY

"Use failure as a motivation tool not as a sign of defeat"

Date: /   /

THINGS TO BE GRATEFUL FOR TODAY

"Never let your dreams die for fear of failure,
defeat is just temporary; your dreams are your power"

Date: /   /

_____

_____

_____

_____

_____

_____

_____

_____

_____

_____

_____

_____

_____

_____

_____

_____

_____

THINGS TO BE GRATEFUL FOR TODAY

"A failure is a lesson, not a loss. It is a temporary and sometimes necessary detour, not a dead end"

Date: /   /

_____
_____
_____
_____
_____
_____
_____
_____
_____
_____
_____
_____
_____
_____
_____
_____

THINGS TO BE GRATEFUL FOR TODAY

"Have faith in the future but above all in yourself"

Date: /   /

_____

_____

_____

_____

_____

_____

_____

_____

_____

_____

_____

_____

_____

_____

_____

_____

_____

THINGS TO BE GRATEFUL FOR TODAY

"Those who live in the past limit their future"
- Anonymous

Date: /   /

_____
_____
_____
_____
_____
_____
_____
_____
_____
_____
_____
_____
_____
_____
_____
_____
_____

THINGS TO BE GRATEFUL FOR TODAY

Date: /   /

_____

_____

_____

_____

_____

_____

_____

_____

_____

_____

_____

_____

_____

_____

_____

THINGS TO BE GRATEFUL FOR TODAY

"Never let your doubt blind your goals, for your future lies in your ability, not your failure" — *Anonymous*

Date: /   /

_____

_____

_____

_____

_____

_____

_____

_____

_____

_____

_____

_____

_____

_____

_____

_____

THINGS TO BE GRATEFUL FOR TODAY

"Don't go into something to test the waters, go into things to make waves" — Anonymous

Date: /   /

THINGS TO BE GRATEFUL FOR TODAY

"Laughter is the shock absorber that softens and minimizes the bumps of life" — Anonymous

Date: /   /

THINGS TO BE GRATEFUL FOR TODAY

"Dream – Believe – Achieve"

Date: /   /

THINGS TO BE GRATEFUL FOR TODAY

"Make your own destiny. Don't wait for it to come to you, life is not a rehearsal" — *Anonymous*

Date: /   /

THINGS TO BE GRATEFUL FOR TODAY

"If you want to feel rich, just count all the things you have that money can't buy" — Anonymous

Date: /   /

THINGS TO BE GRATEFUL FOR TODAY

"Never give up on a dream just because of the time it will take to accomplish it. The time will pass anyway." – Anonymous

Date: /   /

_____
_____
_____
_____
_____
_____
_____
_____
_____
_____
_____
_____
_____
_____
_____
_____
_____
_____

THINGS TO BE GRATEFUL FOR TODAY

Date: /   /

_____

_____

_____

_____

_____

_____

_____

_____

_____

_____

_____

_____

_____

_____

_____

THINGS TO BE GRATEFUL FOR TODAY

"Your only limitation is your imagination" — *Anonymous*

Date: /   /

_____

_____

_____

_____

_____

_____

_____

_____

_____

_____

_____

_____

_____

_____

_____

_____

_____

THINGS TO BE GRATEFUL FOR TODAY

Date: /   /

_____

_____

_____

_____

_____

_____

_____

_____

_____

_____

_____

_____

_____

_____

_____

THINGS TO BE GRATEFUL FOR TODAY

Date: /   /

THINGS TO BE GRATEFUL FOR TODAY

Date: /   /

THINGS TO BE GRATEFUL FOR TODAY

"Never let defeat have the last word" — Anonymous

Date: /   /

_____

_____

_____

_____

_____

_____

_____

_____

_____

_____

_____

_____

_____

_____

_____

_____

_____

THINGS TO BE GRATEFUL FOR TODAY

"The winner always has a plan; The loser always has an excuse" — Anonymous

Date: /   /

THINGS TO BE GRATEFUL FOR TODAY

> *"There is no elevator to success.*
> *You have to take the stairs"* — Anonymous

Date: /   /

THINGS TO BE GRATEFUL FOR TODAY

"Don't let yesterday's disappointments, overshadow tomorrow's achievements" — *Anonymous*

Date: /   /

_____

_____

_____

_____

_____

_____

_____

_____

_____

_____

_____

_____

_____

_____

_____

_____

THINGS TO BE GRATEFUL FOR TODAY

"We are limited, not by our abilities, but by our vision"
— Anonymous

Date: /   /

_____

_____

_____

_____

_____

_____

_____

_____

_____

_____

_____

_____

_____

_____

_____

_____

THINGS TO BE GRATEFUL FOR TODAY

> *"Dreams don't come true. Dreams are true"*
> — Anonymous

Date: /   /

THINGS TO BE GRATEFUL FOR TODAY

> *"Happiness is not something you get,*
> *but something you do"* — Anonymous

Date: /   /

_____

_____

_____

_____

_____

_____

_____

_____

_____

_____

_____

_____

_____

_____

_____

_____

_____

THINGS TO BE GRATEFUL FOR TODAY

> *"A journey of a thousand miles must begin with a single step."* — Lao Tzu

Date: /   /

_____

_____

_____

_____

_____

_____

_____

_____

_____

_____

_____

_____

_____

_____

_____

_____

THINGS TO BE GRATEFUL FOR TODAY

"Try and fail, but don't fail to try" — *Anonymous*

Date: / /

THINGS TO BE GRATEFUL FOR TODAY

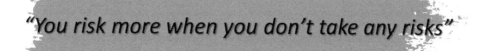

"You risk more when you don't take any risks"

Date: /   /

_____

_____

_____

_____

_____

_____

_____

_____

_____

_____

_____

_____

_____

_____

_____

_____

THINGS TO BE GRATEFUL FOR TODAY

> *"A diamond is a chunk of coal that made good under pressure"* — Anonymous

Date: /   /

THINGS TO BE GRATEFUL FOR TODAY

> *"No dreamer is ever too small; no dream is ever too big."* — Anonymous

Date: /   /

THINGS TO BE GRATEFUL FOR TODAY

"All our tomorrows depend on today" — *Anonymous*

Date: /   /

THINGS TO BE GRATEFUL FOR TODAY

Date:　　/　　/

THINGS TO BE GRATEFUL FOR TODAY

"Dream is not what you see in sleep, dream is the thing which does not let you sleep" — Anonymous

Date: ___ / ___ / ___

_____

_____

_____

_____

_____

_____

_____

_____

_____

_____

_____

_____

_____

_____

_____

_____

_____

_____

_____

THINGS TO BE GRATEFUL FOR TODAY

Date: /   /

_____

_____

_____

_____

_____

_____

_____

_____

_____

_____

_____

_____

_____

_____

_____

_____

THINGS TO BE GRATEFUL FOR TODAY

Date: /   /

_____

THINGS TO BE GRATEFUL FOR TODAY

> *"Once you have a dream put all your heart and soul to achieve it"*

Date: /   /

_____

_____

_____

_____

_____

_____

_____

_____

_____

_____

_____

_____

_____

_____

_____

_____

THINGS TO BE GRATEFUL FOR TODAY

"Follow your heart and your dreams will come true"
— Anonymous

Date: /   /

_____

_____

_____

_____

_____

_____

_____

_____

_____

_____

_____

_____

_____

_____

_____

_____

_____

_____

THINGS TO BE GRATEFUL FOR TODAY

Date: /   /

_____

_____
_____
_____
_____
_____
_____
_____
_____
_____
_____
_____
_____
_____
_____
_____
_____
_____

THINGS TO BE GRATEFUL FOR TODAY

Date: /   /

_____
_____
_____
_____
_____
_____
_____
_____
_____
_____
_____
_____
_____
_____
_____
_____
_____
_____

THINGS TO BE GRATEFUL FOR TODAY

"Difficult roads often lead to beautiful destinations"

Date: /   /

THINGS TO BE GRATEFUL FOR TODAY

"The road to success is always full of surprises and temporary failures, real success comes to those who persist"

Date: /   /

_____
_____
_____
_____
_____
_____
_____
_____
_____
_____
_____
_____
_____
_____
_____
_____
_____
_____
_____

THINGS TO BE GRATEFUL FOR TODAY

"Believe in yourself and you will be unstoppable"

Date: /   /

_____

_____

_____

_____

_____

_____

_____

_____

_____

_____

_____

_____

_____

_____

_____

_____

THINGS TO BE GRATEFUL FOR TODAY

"Today is another chance to get better"

Date: /   /

_____

_____

_____

_____

_____

_____

_____

_____

_____

_____

_____

_____

_____

_____

_____

_____

THINGS TO BE GRATEFUL FOR TODAY

Date: /   /

THINGS TO BE GRATEFUL FOR TODAY

Date: /   /

THINGS TO BE GRATEFUL FOR TODAY

> *"If you do what you always did,*
> *you will get what you always got"* - Anonymous

Date: /   /

_____

_____

_____

_____

_____

_____

_____

_____

_____

_____

_____

_____

_____

_____

_____

_____

_____

THINGS TO BE GRATEFUL FOR TODAY

> *"It's not what you look at that matters,*
> *it's what you see" - Anonymous*

Date: /   /

THINGS TO BE GRATEFUL FOR TODAY

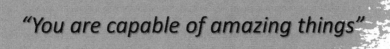

"You are capable of amazing things"

Date: ___ / ___ / ___

THINGS TO BE GRATEFUL FOR TODAY

"Believe in yourself and you will be unstoppable"

Date: /   /

_____

_____

_____

_____

_____

_____

_____

_____

_____

_____

_____

_____

_____

_____

_____

THINGS TO BE GRATEFUL FOR TODAY

> *"Successful people make a habit of doing what unsuccessful people don't want to do"*
> *— Anonymous*

Date: /   /

_____

_____

_____

_____

_____

_____

_____

_____

_____

_____

_____

_____

_____

_____

_____

_____

_____

_____

THINGS TO BE GRATEFUL FOR TODAY

> *"To be the best you must be able
> to handle the worst"* - Anonymous

Date: /   /

_____

_____

_____

_____

_____

_____

_____

_____

_____

_____

_____

_____

_____

_____

_____

_____

_____

_____

THINGS TO BE GRATEFUL FOR TODAY

"Nothing worth having comes easy" - Anonymous

Date: /   /

_____

_____

_____

_____

_____

_____

_____

_____

_____

_____

_____

_____

_____

_____

_____

_____

_____

_____

THINGS TO BE GRATEFUL FOR TODAY

"Follow your dreams, they know the way"

Date: /   /

_____

_____

_____

_____

_____

_____

_____

_____

_____

_____

_____

_____

_____

_____

_____

_____

_____

_____

THINGS TO BE GRATEFUL FOR TODAY

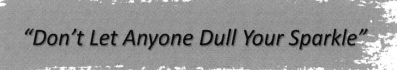

"Don't Let Anyone Dull Your Sparkle"

Date: / /

THINGS TO BE GRATEFUL FOR TODAY

We hope you liked your journal – notebook,
please let us know if you liked it by writing a
review, it means a lot to us.

Thank you!

DESIGNED BY Creative PositivePress FOR:

CREATIVE JOURNALS FACTORY

Made in United States
Orlando, FL
14 May 2022

17853948R00061